Celebrating Christmas

The Life, Times, & Music Series

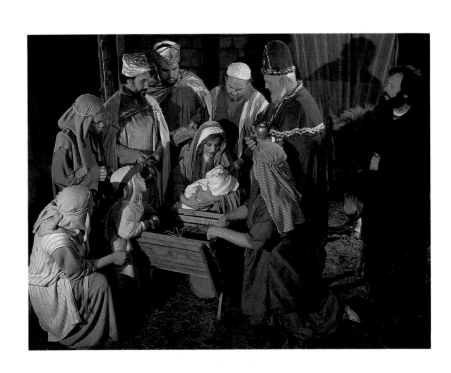

Celebrating Christmas

The Life, Times, & Music Series

Carol Spier

Friedman/Fairfax Publishers

A FRIEDMAN/FAIRFAX BOOK

ISBN 0-9627134-8-1

THE LIFE, TIMES, & MUSIC SERIES: CELEBRATING CHRISTMAS
was prepared and produced by
Friedman/Fairfax Publishers
15 West 26th Street
New York, New York 10010

Editor: Nathaniel Marunas
Art Director: Jeff Batzli
Photography Editor: Grace How
Production Director: Karen Matsu Greenberg

Designed by Zemsky Design

Printed in the United States of America

Contents

Part Two

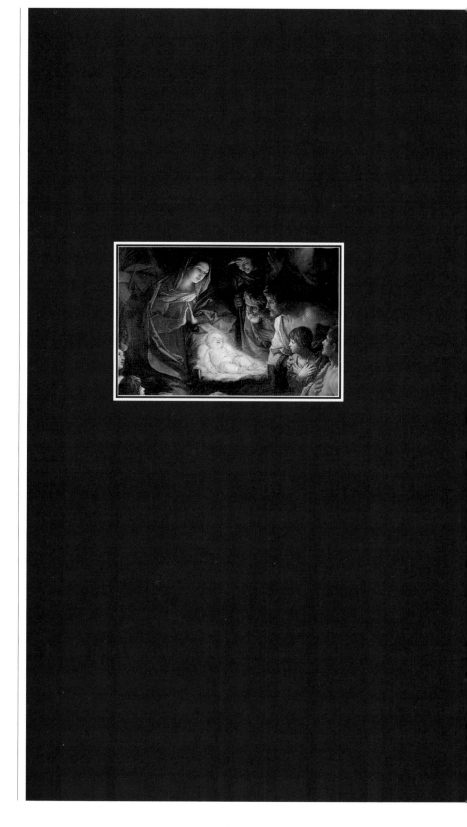

A Short History of the Christmas Celebration

Introduction

Today it is difficult to imagine the celebration of Christmas without music, greenery, gift giving, feasting, and merriment. There is no doubt an element of commercialism in our late-twentieth-century Christmas, and some of the religious observances are overlooked in favor of more secular revelries. In light of the history of the holiday, however, this is not suprising; the celebration of Christmas honors the birth of Christ, but its roots lie in pre-Christian midwinter festivities.

A seventeenth-century portrayal of the Nativity by Guido Reni.

The Origins of the Celebration

The history of Christmas celebrations must therefore include a brief review of various pagan celebrations of the winter solstice. The exact date of the birth of Jesus is unknown, but has always been associated with this season. During the last two millennia, there have been attempts to separate the honoring of Christ's birth from "pagan" customs—to repress the song, dance, and revelry, and to imbue the day with proper and sometimes severe solemnity—but over time many of the ancient customs have been adapted and overlaid with Christian meanings. The conflict between life-affirming pagan celebrations and upholding a stern Christian doctrine has softened, and today Christmas is a festive holiday for all who celebrate it.

The study of festivals and celebrations is fascinating; it reveals customs of remarkable similarity in diverse parts of the world. One important element common to most festive celebrations is song. At Christmastime it is the carol that perhaps best embodies the spirit of the holiday, combining sentiments of faith and the season in a voice that is accessible to all. Examining the history of Christmas highlights the unique and joyful place that carols hold in its celebration.

The Winter Solstice

The winter solstice marks the turning of the seasons, when the days begin to lengthen and the sun begins to climb higher in the sky. It is a universally significant time of year, as it follows the harvest season and precedes the spring. In northern areas, where the harsh climate prevents winter grazing, the harvest often included a slaughter of the animals. This in turn created a sudden abundance of food that certainly contributed to the feasting and celebration that followed. These various harvest festivals were celebrated throughout Europe; evergreens, which are a symbol of fertility or enduring life, and firelight often had symbolic importance in these seasonal rituals.

Above: An engraving depicting Saturnalian revelers. The rule of Saturn was commemorated by the Romans as a long-ago age of peace and happiness.

Right: The wondrous attributes of mistletoe dictated a ceremonial harvest. Pliny the Elder recorded that the Druids cut it with a golden sickle and caught it in a white cloth, ensuring that it never touched the ground.

Saturnalia

In Roman times the feast of the Saturnalia lasted from December 17 to December 24. The festival commemorated the rule of Saturn and was a time of general merry-making characterized by the mingling of the classes, the exchange of gifts, the electing of a mock "king," proscription from normal work, and gambling and drunkenness.

Kalends

On January 1, New Year's Day, new Roman Consuls were inducted into office. The Kalends was an occasion of feasting for wealthy and poor alike, a time when all men became spendthrifts and enjoyed themselves to excess without fear of reprisal. Houses were decorated with greenery; there were candlelit processions with singing; and some people dressed in animal skins or masks. People were expected to give gifts to the emperor, and gifts were also exchanged between common citizens. The Kalends was celebrated throughout the Roman Empire into the twelfth century despite efforts throughout the early Christian era and early Middle Ages to forbid such pagan celebrations. Many European languages include words associated with Christmas that are based upon the Latin kalends.

When Jesus was born a bright star guided the three Magi to Bethlehem.

December 25/ Natalis solis invicti

The winter solstice was established as December 25 by the Julian calendar (introduced in Rome 46 B.C.). The Roman Emperor Aurelian established December 25 as the birthday of the unconquered sun, *Natalis solis invicti*, in A.D. 274. Early Church authorities were aware of these conflicting festivals and that some Christians were participating in them; it appears that when, some time before A.D. 336, they established the commemoration of the birth of Jesus Christ on the 25th of December, they hoped to transfer the celebrations from worship of the sun to worship of the son of God.

The Christmas Story

The story of the birth of Christ is of course central to the celebration of Christmas; it is told with eloquence in the New Testament, as well as in legend. Much scholarly research has been done to determine the dates and locations of the events commonly included in this tale, which is as follows:

In the days of Augustus Caesar the oppressive King Herod governed the land of Israel for Rome. It had been prophesied that the Jews who lived there would someday be delivered by a Messiah, the son of God, who would be born of a virgin in the town of Bethlehem.

Joseph, a carpenter and a descendant of King David, lived in Nazareth and was engaged to a young woman named Mary. Before they were married the angel Gabriel appeared before Mary and told her that she would bear the son of God. When Joseph learned that Mary was expecting a child he wanted at first to hide her from shame. The angel appeared to Joseph to assure him that they should be married, that Mary bore the son of God, who would save his people from their sins, and that when the child was born he should be called Jesus.

Shortly before the child was due the Emperor decreed that all citizens must go to their cities to pay a tax, so Joseph and Mary journeyed to Bethlehem in compliance. Once there, they found that all the inns were full, and they were forced to lodge in a stable, where the child was born. Mary wrapped the infant in swaddling clothes and laid him in a manger.

A star appeared in the heavens to signal the birth of the Infant Jesus. Angels spread the word and people came to pay their respects. Shepherds came from nearby fields, offering whatever they had as gifts. The animals gathered around and there was singing in the air.

16

Representations of the Nativity range from simple to ornate.

The star appeared to three wise kings (or Magi) and they followed it. When they reached Jerusalem they asked Herod where the child was. One of the prophesies concerning the birth of Christ had been that He would rule the people of Israel. Herod had been made nervous by the reports of this event and asked the Magi to go to Bethlehem, find the child, and return to tell him of its where-abouts so that he could worship it as well.

January 6th, the Twelfth Day (or Night) after Christmas, the Epiphany, commemorates the baptism of Christ and the adoration of the Magi. They carried gifts for the child that were prophetic: Melchior, King of Arabia, brought a gold casket in the form of a shrine, symbolizing the king that Jesus would become; Caspar, King of Tarsus, brought myrrh in a gold-mounted horn, symbolizing the physician; Balthazar, King of Ethiopia, brought frankincense, symbolizing the high priest.

After finding the infant, the Magi were warned in a dream not to return to Herod, so they journeyed back to their own lands by other routes. In time, when the Magi did not return to him, Herod decreed that all infants under a certain age in and around Bethlehem should be killed. But an angel warned Joseph of this so he, Mary, and Jesus fled to Egypt to wait until it was safe for them to return.

Greenery

Evergreens are an age-old symbol of survival that from ancient times have been associated with midwinter festivals. The custom of decorating with evergreens has links to various magical rites and spiritual beliefs; many pagan peoples thought that evergreens had protective and life-renewing qualities. Bringing evergreens indoors was a way to provide a winter refuge for vegetation spirits, while carrying them in a procession was believed to disperse their protective magic over all they passed.

Opposite page, top: Some attribute the first lighted Christmas tree to Martin Luther. Opposite page, below: This Christmas tree in Rockefeller Center, New York, is a testament to the importance of evergreens. Below, bottom: The hanging of evergreens has accompanied midwinter festivities for millennia.

WITH THE YEAR'S BLESSING IN ATTENDANCE.

The Christmas Tree

The custom of decorating a fir tree at Christmas probably derives from an early effort to impose Christian symbolism on surviving pagan customs. It may have originated in eighth-century Germany when St. Boniface, to supplant folk-worship of the oak, dedicated the fir tree to the Holy Child. In a parallel custom in some parts of Germany, wooden pyramids were set up and decorated with greens, Nativity figures, and candles.

December 24 was once considered the day of Adam and Eve; medieval mystery plays depicting their story featured "paradise trees" — evergreens hung with apples. As Christmas was celebrated on what had been the birthday of the sun, and as candles had been symbols of the sun's power during the Roman Saturnalia, bringing lights to the tree was a natural next step. There is another legend that holds that the splendor of a particularly clear and starry Christmas Eve sky inspired Martin Luther to fill a tree with candles as an image of the heavens from which Christ was sent.

Whatever its provenance, decorating a Christmas tree in the manner that we know today did not become a universal custom until the middle of the nineteenth century, when Queen Victoria and Prince Albert's elaborate tree was reproduced in newspaper illustrations. By the 1870s the manufacture of ornaments was a considerable business, particularly in Germany, and decorative electric lights were introduced around the turn of the century.

Holly, Ivy, and Mistletoe

Although evergreen decorations are holdovers from pagan days, they are commonplace today even in places of worship. The fertility symbolism of evergreens has had other imagery superimposed upon it—the blood of Christ in particular is associated with the red berries of holly. In some places it is considered unlucky to bring evergreens into the house before Christmas Eve, and there are various superstitions about how long they should be left up and how they must be disposed of (usually burnt or fed to the animals, but rarely thrown away).

Holly also carries a number of sexual connotations, and "The Holly and the Ivy" is not the only early carol that portrays holly in masculine counterpart to the feminine ivy. Another tradition holds that the prickly varieties are masculine (in keeping with the rougher nature of the male animal) while the smooth are feminine. If prickly holly is brought into the house the husband will rule during the next year; if smooth, the wife.

This charming illustration from the December 25, 1889, Harper's Weekly, shows young people fashioning masses of greenery into wreaths.

The legends surrounding mistletoe are more complex. It has always been invested with magic qualities because it is green and fruit-bearing in winter and does not root in the ground but grows semi-parasitically on trees. (In fact, the birds that eat mistletoe berries imbed them in the bark of the tree, causing new plants to sprout.) European mistletoe grows on oak trees, which are themselves sacred in many cultures. Many people believed that mistletoe, probably because of its curious method of growth, cured sterility and epilepsy and was an antidote to poison.

The exact origin of kissing under the mistletoe is unknown, but doubtless has some connections with its early fertility symbolism. Early mistletoe balls were quite elaborate: several hoops were joined to make a sphere that was covered with ivy and hung with ribbons and fruit; Nativity figures usually sat or hung inside it; and a small bunch of mistletoe, which was not plentiful, hung beneath.

21

The Yule Fire

Midwinter fires and lights are ancient symbols of everlasting life and the return of the sun to full power. Many early midwinter festivals involved sacrificial fires, and the custom of keeping a fire burning on the hearth at Christmas is connected to the belief that the hearth is a place where ancestral spirits come back to communicate with the living. There are different traditions surrounding the Yule log; in some places it must be oak, in some fruit wood. There is usually some ceremony connected with bringing the log into the house: sometimes it must be lit with the embers of the last year's log, sometimes money is placed on the log, and sometimes the lighting is accompanied by the drinking of wine. Some believe that bad luck will come to a house where the fire is allowed to go out at Christmas, and no one will give burning embers to a neighbor whose log has gone out. The ashes of the yule log must be disposed of properly. In some places they are used to purify wells, protect against hail or lightning, or to perform other mystical duties.

Two renderings of the celebratory festivities associated with bringing in the Yule log.

The Story of Saint Nicholas

Saint Nicholas was a fourth-century Bishop of Myra in Asia Minor who was reputed to have been extremely kind, especially to children; he is the patron saint of boys. He brings holiday gifts to children—traditionally, fruit and sweet things for good children and rods for the bad—in some parts of Europe on December 5, the eve of his feast day, in others on Christmas Eve. Children put out their shoes, filled with hay or a carrot for the Saint's horse, before they go to bed, and when they awaken they find the shoes filled with gifts.

During the Reformation the worship of saints was forbidden, so Saint Nicholas was transformed into Father Nicholas. In England, Saint Nicholas became Father Christmas; in Holland he became Sinterklaas, who in turn became the American Santa Claus. While the European Saint Nicholas is usually thin and stately, his American counterpart is round and rosy-cheeked, a characterization established in the poem "A Visit from St. Nicholas," written by Clement Moore in 1822 and illustrated in 1863 for *Harper's Weekly* by political cartoonist Thomas Nast.

The custom of hanging stockings is also derived from an act of Saint Nicholas. Legend holds that in the fourth century there was an impoverished nobleman who despaired of finding dowries for his three lovely daughters. The beneficent Saint rode by their home one evening and saw that the girls, who were good homemakers, had hung their freshly laundered clothing by the fire to dry overnight. The Saint dropped gold coins down the chimney, and when the daughters awoke they found their stockings filled and their futures assured.

Opposite page: One of Thomas Nast's numerous depictions of "Merry Old Santa Claus." Above: A contemporary mantel hung with stockings. Below: Antique Santa gift tags.

A Very Happy Christmas

· THE · WAITS ·

WE COME A·SINGING TO YOUR GATES,
SO LISTEN AT YOUR LEISURE!
WE ARE THE MERRY CHRISTMAS WAITS,
WHO WISH YOU PEACE & PLEASURE!

Christmas Gifts and Cards

The custom of exchanging gifts at Christmas is linked to the New Year's gifts first exchanged during

Above: A charming illustration of costumed young waits singing out their holiday greetings. Below: Gift giving — an aspect of Christmas that dates back to the Saturnalia. Opposite page: A Christmas tree — the archetypal greenery associated with the season.

the Kalends; to the gifts brought to the Christ Child; and to Saint Nicholas. Like the Christmas tree, Christmas cards came into common use in the nineteenth century, when the mass production of multicolored cards became possible.

Carols, Dancing, and the Creche

Carols can generally be defined as joyous, simple songs written in vernacular language and most often having a religious impulse. There is no specific musical form that a carol must follow, although they very often contain verses separated by a repeated refrain. They are generally meant to be performed by a solo voice, accompanied by a chorus and simple musical instruments. Some carols are secular, and many are not joyous, but somber. On the whole, carols are emotional songs that are accessible to all. They are traditionally associated with many religious festivals and it is only within the last two hundred years that they have become primarily associated with the Christmas season.

The carols we sing today come from all over Europe and the New World, though the provenance of some is unknown or incomplete. Many traditional carols have been known in several forms; old verses have been matched with new tunes and vice versa; folk songs have been reworded to give their imagery properly spiritual meanings; and Latin and vernacular hymns have been translated and transformed into carols. Clergymen of many denominations have written both words and music to carols, and poets and composers of no particular faith have also done so.

Carols did not become closely connected to the Church until the fifteenth century. Indeed, early Church authorities repressed dance and revelry because of their pagan associations. Religious music primarily took the form of plainsong or unaccompanied chant.

In the Middle Ages, several things influenced the ways of worship and the development of Western music, including the carol: the rise of minstrels and troubadours; the life of Saint Francis; and the development of miracle and mystery plays.

Jongleurs, Minstrels, and Troubadours

Jongleurs were wandering performers who appeared sometime around the tenth century. They sang and danced, but also did acrobatics and kept trained animals. Social outcasts, they earned a precarious living wandering from town to town, performing alone or in small groups.

By the thirteenth century, these wandering musicians evolved into trained professional performers called minstrels. Troubadours, on the other hand, were poet-composers of the knightly class, and were not necessarily performers; their works often celebrated love, whether courtly, earthly, or illicit. Waits were town minstrels who were

Sixteenth-century midwinter revelers in a pageant of celebration.

responsible for keeping watch in the streets at night and for calling out the hours. They sometimes worked in groups and evolved into the early bands of strolling carolers who "went awassailing."

Though few could read music, minstrels were expected to play a variety of instruments. In the fourteenth century they began to organize into guilds, which, among other things, provided musical training and hospices for members, and built churches. In the fifteenth century, music changed so that musicians were required to specialize on a particular instrument. At this time the term minstrel, which continued to mean a nonspecialized performer, assumed a negative connotation. For the time that they flourished, minstrels were very important in popularizing secular music, and some of the tunes that they played may have been later matched with carol words.

Saint Francis

Saint Francis is credited by many as the father of the carol and mystery and miracle plays. He transformed a stern religion with a judgmental Christ into a tender one that depicted life on Earth as the story of the brotherhood of all mankind.

Francis lived in the thirteenth century, a time when most common people could not read or write (and long before the invention of the printing press). In 1224, in an effort to make the story of the birth of Christ more accessible, Francis had a manger scene built in the church, complete with ox and ass, and while people viewed it by torchlight, Francis preached the story and sang. It was a moving and spiritual evening filled with joy, and the custom of recreating the crib continues today.

Miracle and Mystery Plays

Miracle plays were Medieval religious dramatizations staged by the clergy in Latin; mystery plays depicted stories from the Bible and miracle plays dramatized those of the lives of the saints. Over time these plays were translated to the vernacular

A contemporary enactment of the Nativity.

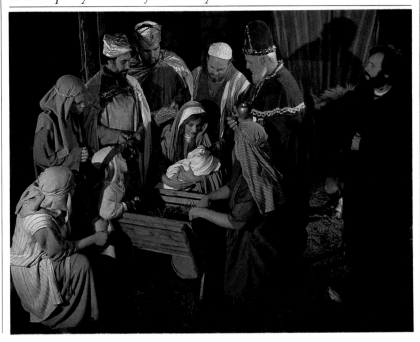

by the different trade guilds and contained a mixture of religious and secular material and song— not to mention coarse buffoonery. (The Nativity was a frequent theme and "The Coventry Carol" is from such a play.)

The Fifteenth Century

The first known carols appeared in the fifteenth century, a period of great religious songwriting in Germany and France. This was the time when the miracle and mystery plays reached the peak of their popularity; much of the music in them was based on folk tunes and the words were sung in the vernacular. After centuries of repression, the joy that was inherent in festive singing was recognized and incorporated into Church practices; at last the carol had lost its pagan connotation.

Some of the early carols derive from the miracle plays and some contain imagery that is far older, such as the yule log, boar's head, and holly and ivy, while others reflect aspects of rural life in the Middle Ages. Some carols were written entirely in the vernacular; some, known as macaronic, contain vernacular verse interspersed with Latin phrases (usually from familiar hymns).

The Reformation

The carol held its festive importance through the sixteenth and into the seventeenth century, when the more extreme factions (in England and the New World, particularly) of the Reformation suppressed it and many other observations of Christmas as pagan or Romish. During this time caroling was kept alive by oral tradition and the distribution of a handful of printed broadsheets.

The Eighteenth Century

Musically, the eighteenth century is of the utmost importance, encompassing as it does the great Baroque and early Classical periods. There was a slight revival of interest in carols during this period, and some new ones were written, most notably "Hark the Herald Angels Sing" (1738) by Charles Wesley, brother of John Wesley, the founder of Methodism. (This song, written as a hymn, was originally set to another tune. We now sing it to a Mendelssohn air that was composed in 1848 to commemorate the invention of printing. While Mendelssohn thought the tune potentially popular he felt it would be inappropriate in a religious context. After his death, a pupil of his adapted the words of the hymn to the music.)

The Nineteenth Century

It was not until the nineteenth century that a serious effort was made to rediscover the traditional carols that had been suppressed during the Reformation. The nineteenth century was characterized by great social change accompanied by a movement among scholars to collect and document folklore before it was lost. Two men independently collected and published traditional carols: Davies Gilbert, in 1822 and again in 1823, and William

Sandys, in 1833. Over the next few decades other collections of carols, as well as other folk music, were published.

In the middle of the century the Oxford Movement within the Church of England revived traditional rituals and music in the high church. Dr. John Mason Neale translated, rewrote, modernized, and published many of the carols and songs contained in *Piae Cantiones,* a rare Swedish Lutheran book published in 1582. He then published an inexpensive edition for use by the general pub-

lic. There is considerable scholarly debate as to the actual merit of his work, some of the modernizations now being judged inferior to the beauty of the original pieces, but there is no doubt that he played a crucial role in giving new legitimacy to the carol.

This renewal of interest in carols was just one of the things that helped to shape Christmas into the holiday that we celebrate today: Charles Dickens published *A Christmas Carol* in 1843, which did much to instill a spirit of generosity and good will into the season; Queen Victoria and Prince Albert popularized the decorated tree; ornaments were mass produced in Germany and exported throughout Europe and to America; and the Christmas card became common. As technology has advanced and the world has become smaller (so to speak), Christmas has become more and more a holiday that is embraced by families all over the world.

A nineteenth-century illustration showing children caroling in a rural area. If they were following the wassail tradition, they would have expected food, drink, or money in return for their songs.

34

The Carols
and
Their Stories

Introduction

What is known of the provenance of the carols on this disc is included here, along with the lyrics. At the end of this section is a rough chronology of the carols that should help to place them within the context of the background information given in the first section of the book.

Twelfth night revelers in the seventeenth century.

The First Nowell

he first printed copies of this carol date from 1822 and 1833, but the tune itself is a traditional one that *The Oxford Book of Carols* dates as "not later than the seventeenth century." It is thought to be of either French or English origin. "Nowell" is derived from the French "Noël" (or Christmas). This particular carol describes the star that guided the three Magi to the Christ Child and as such is appropriate for Epiphany. The refrain is repeated after each verse.

Angels spread the joyous news of the Nativity as illustrated in this engraving of a work by P. Lagarde.

The first Nowell the angel did say,
Was to certain poor shepherds in fields as they lay,
In fields where they lay keeping their sheep,
On a cold winter's night that was so deep.

Nowell, Nowell, Nowell, Nowell,
Born is the King of Israel.

They looked up and saw a star
Shining in the east, beyond them far;
And to the earth it gave great light,
And so it continued both day and night.

And by the light of that same star,
Three wise men came from country far;
To seek for a king was their intent,
And to follow the star wherever it went.

This star drew nigh to the northwest,
O'er Bethlehem it took its rest,
And there it did both stop and stay
Right over the place where Jesus lay.

Then entered in those wise men three,
Full rev'rently upon their knee,
And offer'd there, in his presence,
Their gold, and myrrh, and frankincense.

Then let us all with one accord
Sing praises to our heav'nly Lord,
That hath made heav'n and earth of nought
And with his blood mankind hath bought.

O Christmas Tree

 lmost nothing is known of this traditional and extremely popular German song "O Tannenbaum." It probably originated in Westphalia and the tune may be that of an old Catholic hymn. (It is also interesting to note that this tune is the same as the state song of Maryland, "Maryland, My Maryland.")

A tree with a mix of contemporary and antique decorations.

O Christmas tree, O Christmas tree,
O tree of green unchanging.
O Christmas tree, O Christmas tree,
O tree of green unchanging.

Your boughs are green in summertime;
To greet the snows of wintertime.

O Christmas tree, O Christmas tree,
O tree of green unchanging.

O Christmas tree, O Christmas tree,
You set my heart a-singing.
O Christmas tree, O Christmas tree,
You set my heart a-singing.

Like little stars, your candles bright,
Send to the world a wondrous light.

O Christmas tree, O Christmas tree,
You set my heart a-singing.

O Christmas tree, O Christmas tree,
You come from God eternal.
O Christmas tree, O Christmas tree,
You come from God eternal.

A symbol of the Lord of love,
Put on the earth, sent from above.

O Christmas tree, O Christmas tree,
You come from God eternal.

What Child Is This

his hymn was penned by William Dix, a Victorian insurance executive who wrote hymns as a pastime. Originally written in 1878, these verses were first matched to a tune in 1878 in a song called "The Manger Throne." Sometime later the words were found to fit perfectly with the old English tune "Greensleeves." The first reference to this tune dates from 1580, when a license to print it was issued. For those who are interested, the lyrics appear below.

A very charming Victorian Christmas card of the type made possible by the invention of chromolithography.

What child is this, who, laid to rest,
On Mary's lap is sleeping?
Whom angels greet with anthems sweet,
While shepherds watch are keeping?
This, this is Christ the King,
Whom shepherds guard and angels sing!
Haste, haste to bring him laud,
The babe, the son of Mary!

Why lies he in such mean estate,
Where ox and ass are feeding?
Good Christian, fear, for sinners here
The silent Word is pleading.
Nails, spear shall pierce him through,
The cross be born for me, for you.
Hail, hail, the Word made flesh,
The babe, the son of Mary!

So bring him incense, gold, and myrrh;
Come peasant, king, to own him.
The King of Kings salvation brings;
Let loving hearts enthrone him.
Raise, raise the song on high!
The Virgin sings her lullaby.
Joy, joy, for Christ is born,
The babe, the son of Mary!

Lo, How a Rose

And there shall come forth a rod out of the stem of Jesse, and a branch shall grow out of his roots. (Isaiah 11:1)

With these words Isaiah prophesied the birth of Jesus. The plant imagery connected with the Nativity was extended to include wondrous tales of various trees and shrubs bursting into bloom on Christmas Eve and these verses can be interpreted both literally and metaphorically. The phrase "when half spent was the night" is a reference to midwinter, the darkest time of year, as well as to midnight.

This carol is quite old; the melody dates from the sixteenth century and was first printed with the (perhaps older) words in German around 1600. Michael Praetorius, a German composer and music theorist, harmonized the tune in 1609. The verses were translated into English in the nineteenth century.

Adoration of the Magi by the fifteenth-century painter Fra Filippo Lippi.

Lo, how a rose e'er blooming
From tender stem has sprung?
Of Jesse's lineage coming
As men of old have sung.
It came, a flow'ret bright,
Amid the cold of winter,
When half spent was the night.

Isaiah 'twas foretold it,
The rose I had in mind;
With Mary we behold it,
The Virgin mother kind.
To show God's love aright
She bore to men a Savior,
When half spent was the night.

The Holly and the Ivy

The original symbolism of holly and ivy, which were among the evergreens commonly used in pre-Christian midwinter festivals, was sexual. These plants figure in many old carols, often set in contrast to echo the relationship between men and women. A song of this type was no doubt sung and danced as a dialogue, with men taking the part of Holly and women that of Ivy. In this traditional carol some of the metaphors have been given Christian meanings but much of the old seasonal imagery remains. The "merry organ" was a portable organ similar to the one mentioned in Geoffrey Chaucer's "Nun's Priest's Tale." The refrain is repeated after each verse.

Today, greenery is displayed both in- and out-of-doors at Christmastime.

The holly and the ivy,
When they are both full grown,
Of all the trees that are in the wood,
The holly bears the crown.

O The rising of the sun,
And the running of the deer,
The playing of the merry organ,
Sweet singing in the choir.

The holly bears a blossom
As white as the lily flower;
And Mary bore sweet Jesus Christ
To be our sweet Savior.

The holly bears a berry
As red as any blood;
And Mary bore sweet Jesus Christ
To do poor sinners good.

The holly bears a prickle
As sharp as any thorn
And Mary bore sweet Jesus Christ
On Christmas Day in the morn.

The holly bears a bark
As bitter as any gall
And Mary bore sweet Jesus Christ
For to redeem us all.

Good King Wenceslas

 enceslas the Holy was a Duke of Bohemia who was murdered by his brother in A.D. 936. Wenceslas was renowned for his good deeds, most of which were probably of far more consequence than those celebrated in this song, and he was canonized in the eleventh century. Saint Stephen was the first Christian martyr; his feast day is traditionally held on December 26.

The words of this carol were written by Dr. John Mason Neale for his adaptation of *Piae Cantiones*. Scholars often malign the sentimentality and Victorian morality imposed on what was originally a light and lively (and probably secular) dance tune, but the song has been loved by carolers since it was published in 1853. For those who are interested, the lyrics are presented below.

Good King Wenceslas looked out
On the Feast of Stephen,
When the snow lay round about,
Deep and crisp and even:
Brightly shone the moon that night,
Though the frost was cruel,
When a poor man came in sight,
Gathering winter fuel.

"Hither page, and stand by me,
If thou knows't it, telling,
Yonder peasant, who is he?
Where and what his dwelling?"
"Sire, he lives a good league hence,
Underneath the mountain,
Right against the forest fence,
By Saint Agnes' fountain."

"Bring me flesh, and bring me wine,
Bring me pine logs hither;
Thou and I will see him dine,
When we bear them thither."
Page and monarch forth they went,
Forth they went together,
Through the rude wind's wild lament
And the bitter weather.

"Sire the night is darker now,
And the wind blows stronger;
Fails my heart, I know not how,
I can go no longer."
"Mark my footsteps, good my page,
Tread thou in them boldly:
Thou shalt find the winter's rage
Freeze thy blood less coldly."

In his master's steps he trod,
Where the snow lay dinted;
Heat was in the very sod
Which the saint had printed.
Therefore, Christian men be sure,
Wealth or rank possessing,
Ye who now will bless the poor,
Shall yourselves find blessing.

Coventry Carol

his carol survives from the *Pageant of the Shearman and Tailors* in the Coventry miracle plays. The *Pageant* dates from the fifteenth century; these lullaby verses were written by Robert Croo in 1534 for a scene where the mothers learn of Herod's order to slay the children. The tune dates from 1591. Begin with the refrain and repeat it only after the third verse.

Victorian carolers.

Lully, lulla, thou little tiny child,
By by, lully, lullay.

O sisters, too,
How may we do
For to preserve this day
This poor youngling,
For whom we do sing,
By by, lully, lullay?

Herod, the king,
In his raging,
Charged he hath this day
His men of might,
In his own sight,
All young children to slay.

That woe is me,
Poor child for thee!
And ever morn and day,
For thy parting
Neither say nor sing
By by, lully, lullay!

I Heard The Bells on Christmas Day

 enry Wadsworth Longfellow, the American classics scholar, professor, and poet, wrote these verses in 1863 as a poem entitled "Christmas Bells." He did not intend it to be set to music. Longfellow suffered several personal tragedies during his life and the news that his son, who was a lieutenant in the Army of the Potomac, had been wounded prompted him to write this poem, which had a personal and political relevance now transcended by a more universal yearning for peace on earth.

Bell-ringing merrymakers hard at play.

I heard the bells on Christmas day
Their old familiar carols play
And mild and sweet the words repeat,
Of peace on earth, good will to men.

I thought how as the day had come,
The belfries of all Christendom
Had roll'd along th' unbroken song
Of peace on earth, good will to men.

And in despair I bow'd my head:
"There is no peace on earth," I said,
"For hate is strong, and mocks the song
Of peace on earth, good will to men."

Then pealed the bells more loud and deep:
"God is not dead, nor doth he sleep;
The wrong shall fail, the right prevail,
With peace on earth, good will to men."

The Wassail Song

"assail" comes from the old English "wes hal," meaning good luck or good health. As a noun it refers to a drink (usually a spiced ale that is served hot), as a verb to the activity of singing door-to-door in expectation of refreshment. This carol probably originated in the North of England in the seventeenth century and can be taken quite literally; between Christmas and New Year's Day, groups of local children would go singing and begging from house to house, and they were often rewarded with a cup of wassail. It is easy to see that the caroling must have become increasingly jolly as the singers progressed. The refrain is repeated after each verse.

Depiction of Tudor Christmas festivities.

Here we come awassailing
Among the leaves so green,
Yes, here we come awandering,
So fair to be seen.

Love and joy come to you,
And to you your wassail too,
And God bless you and send you
A happy New Year,
And God send you a happy New Year.

We earn our daily bread
As we go from door to door
But we are neighbor's children
Let round the table go.

We've got a little purse
Of stretching leather skin;
We want a little money
To line it well within.

God bless the master of this house,
Likewise the mistress too;
And all the little children
That round the table go.

Good Master and good Mistress,
While you're sitting by the fire,
Pray think of us poor children
Who wander in the mire.

O Come, All Ye Faithful

deste Fideles, the Latin hymn for Christmas from which these words are translated, has been known since the beginning of the eighteenth century. The tune was most likely written by John Francis Wade, a layman who was a music teacher and copyist; it first appeared in print in 1782. It was translated into English in the middle of the nineteenth century by Frederick Oakley. The refrain is repeated after each verse.

An engraving of the Adoration of the Kings, *by Gentile da Fabriano.*

O come, all ye faithful,
Joyful and triumphant,
O come ye, O come ye to Bethlehem;
Come and behold him
Born the King of angels.

O come, let us adore him,
O come, let us adore him,
O come, let us adore him,
Christ the Lord.

God of God,
Light of light,
Lo! he abhors not the Virgin's womb;
Very God,
Begotten not created:

Sing, choirs of angels,
Sing in exultation,
All ye citizens of heav'n above;
Glory to God
In the highest:

Yea, Lord, we greet thee,
Born this happy morning,
Jesus, to thee be glory giv'n;
Word of the Father,
Now in flesh appearing:

Ave Maria

he original text to this Latin prayer is from the Roman Catholic liturgy, and has been set to various melodies over the years. The tune recorded here was written in 1859 by French composer Charles-François Gounod (1818-1893), and is based on the harmonic structure of the C major Prelude from Book I of the *Well-Tempered Clavier*, by Johann Sebastian Bach (1658-1750).

Below: Detail of the fifteenth-century Adoration of the Magi *by Domenico Ghirlandaio. Opposite page: A painting by V. M. Vasnetzoff of the Madonna and Child that hangs in the Vladimir Cathedral in Kiev.*

O Holy Night

he melody for this carol (known in the original French as "Cantique de Noël") was composed in 1847 by Adolphe Adam, who is known for composing the ballet *Giselle* and several popular operas. The words were written in the same year by Cappeau de Roquemaure, and translated to English by John Sullivan in 1858. The melody is hauntingly beautiful and it has become one of the world's best-loved carols.

Detail from Madonna with Child, Angel and Saint, *by Domenico Ghirlandaio.*

O holy night! the stars are brightly shining,
It is the night of the dear Savior's birth;
Long lay the world in sin and error pining,
Till He appeared and the soul felt its worth.
A thrill of hope, the weary world rejoices,
For yonder breaks a new and glorious morn.
Fall on your knees, O hear the angel voices!
O night divine, O night when Christ was born!
O night divine, O night, O night divine!

Fall on your knees, O hear the angel voices!
O night divine, O night when Christ was born!
O night divine, O night, O night divine!

O Little Town of Bethlehem

he author of these verses was Phillips Brooks, a nineteenth-century American clergyman who became Bishop of Massachusetts. In 1865, when he was thirty, he made a pilgrimage to the Holy Land, where he looked down from a hilltop on the village of Bethlehem. Three years later the memory of the experience inspired him to write a poem, which he gave to Lewis Redner, his organist and Sunday School Superintendent, on a Saturday at Christmastime; Redner had the music ready for the next day's Sunday School service.

The three kings look to the bright star shining over Jesus in Bethlehem.

O little town of Bethlehem,
How still we see thee lie!
Above thy deep and dreamless sleep
The silent stars go by.
Yet in thy dark streets shineth
The everlasting light;
The hopes and fears of all the years
Are met in thee tonight.

For Christ is born of Mary,
And gather'd all above,
While mortals sleep, the angels keep
Their watch of wond'ring love.
O morning stars, together
Proclaim the holy birth,
And praises sing to God the King,
And peace to men on earth.

How silently, how silently,
The wondrous gift is giv'n!
So God imparts to human hearts
The blessings of his heav'n.
No ear may hear his coming;
But in this world of sin,
Where meek souls will receive him still
The dear Christ enters in.

O holy child of Bethlehem,
Descend to us, we pray;
Cast out our sin and enter in,
Be born in us today.
We hear the Christmas angels
The great glad tidings tell:
O come to us, abide with us,
Our Lord Emmanuel.

It Came Upon a Midnight Clear

r. Edmund Sears, the author of these verses, was a Unitarian minister trained at the Harvard Divinity School. He was one of the first preachers to propound "peace on the earth, good will to men" as a central Christian philosophy and his views were considered radical in the middle of the nineteenth century. The poem was published in the *Christian Register* in 1850; the third stanza sometimes has been omitted because of its harsh tone. It is interesting to note the similarities between this poem and Longfellow's "I Heard the Bells on Christmas Day," which was written about fifteen years later.

The tune was written at about the same time by another American, Richard Willis, who was educated at Yale and studied with Felix Mendelssohn. At one time he was the music critic for the *New York Tribune*. He was vestryman at the Little Church Around the Corner in New York City when he composed this carol. Willis intended the tune for some other verses, and several years passed before it was matched with Sears' poem; it is not likely that the two men ever had a chance to meet.

It came upon a midnight clear,
That glorious song of old,
From angels bending near the earth
To touch their harps of gold:
"Peace on the earth good will to men
From heav'n's all-gracious King!"
The world in solemn stillness lay
To hear the angels sing.

Still through the cloven skies they come,
With peaceful wings unfurled;
And still their heav'nly music floats
O'er all the weary world;
Above its sad and lowly plains
They bend on hov'ring wing;
And ever o'er its Babel sounds
The blessed angels sing.

Yet with the woes of sin and strife
The world has suffered long;
Beneath the angel strain have rolled
Two thousand years of wrong;
And man, at war with man, hears not
The love song which they bring:
O hush the noise, ye men of strife,
And hear the angels sing!

For lo! the days are hast'ning on,
By prophet-bards foretold,
When, with the ever-circling years,
Comes round the age of gold.
When peace shall over all the earth
Its ancient splendors fling,
And the whole world send back the song
Which now the angels sing.

We Wish You A Merry Christmas

his is a traditional English carol, very likely sung by the waits as they strolled singing from house-to-house. Like the wassailing children, they would have expected a reward for their performance and may have sung this as their last piece. The refrain is repeated after each verse.

This 1873 woodcut shows a family dancing around a candlelit tree. Electric lights were introduced at the turn of the twentieth century.

We wish you a merry Christmas,
We wish you a merry Christmas,
We wish you a merry Christmas,
And a happy New Year.

Good tidings to you, wherever you are;
Good tidings for Christmas and a happy New Year.

Now bring us some figgy pudding,
Now bring us some figgy pudding,
Now bring us some figgy pudding,
And bring some out here.

For we all like figgy pudding,
For we all like figgy pudding,
For we all like figgy pudding,
So bring some out here.

And we won't go until we get some,
We won't go until we get some,
We won't go until we get some,
So bring some out here.

We wish you a merry Christmas,
We wish you a merry Christmas,
We wish you a merry Christmas
And a happy New Year.

We wish you a merry Christmas
And a happy New Year.

Recommended Reading

This book would not have been possible without access to previous scholarly research. Anyone interested in the history of carols or other, more specific folkloric traditions will find the following of interest:

➤ *A Country Christmas.* Alexandria, VA: Time-Life Books, 1989.

➤ Dearmer, Percy, R. Vaughn Williams, and Martin Shaw. *The Oxford Book of Carols.* London: Oxford University Press, 1964.

➤ Frazer, Sir James George. *The Golden Bough.* New York: Macmillan, 1958.

➤ Miles, Clement A. *Christmas Customs and Traditions.* New York: Dover Publications, 1976.

➤ Morehead, James, and Allen Moorehead. *Best-Loved Songs and Hymns.* New York: Funk & Wagnalls, 1965.

➤ Poston, Elizabeth. *The Penguin Book of Christmas Carols.* Harmondsworth, England: Penguin, 1965.

➤ Simon, Henry W. *Treasury of Christmas Songs and Carols.* Boston: Houghton Mifflin, 1955.

➤ Willcocks, David. *Carols For Christmas.* New York: The Metropolitan Museum of Art and Holt, Rinehart and Winston, 1983.

Photography & Illustration Credits

Index

Chronology of the Carols

The Holly and the Ivy ....Unknown

O Christmas Tree ....Unknown

Good King Wenceslas.............................1500s (words added 1853)

Coventry Carol 1534

Lo, How a Rose 1600s

The Wassail Song...1600s

We Wish You a Merry Christmas 1600s

The First Nowell ....1600s (first printings, 1822 and 1823)

O Come, All Ye Faithful ....1700s (in Latin; translated

to English, 1852)

O Holy Night ....1847 (in French; translated

to English, 1858)

It Came Upon a Midnight Clear 1849

Ave Maria...............................1859 (based on C major Prelude by

J.S. Bach; words from Catholic liturgy)

I Heard The Bells on Christmas Day .....1863 (from a poem by Longfellow)

O Little Town of Bethlehem 1868

What Child Is This................1878 (words originally set to The Manger

Throne; later, to Greensleeves,

which dates from 1580)